The Smiley Face Balloon

The Flamekeeper Series · Book 1

Joe Sanseverino

Copyright © 2025 by Joe Sanseverino
theflamekeeperseries.com

All rights reserved.

No part of this publication may be reproduced, distributed, or transmitted in any form or by any means, including photocopying, recording, or other electronic or mechanical methods, without the prior written permission of the publisher, except in the case of brief quotations embodied in critical reviews and certain other noncommercial uses permitted by copyright law.

This is a work of fiction. Names, characters, places, and incidents are either products of the author's imagination or are used fictitiously. Any resemblance to actual persons, living or dead, businesses, events, or locales is entirely coincidental.

AI image-generation tools were used in the development of illustrations for this book, always under the full authorship and creative direction of the writer.

Publisher's Cataloging-in-Publication Data

Names: Sanseverino, Joe, author.
Title: The smiley face balloon / Joe Sanseverino.
Series: The Flamekeeper Series
Description: Clark, NJ: Joe Sanseverino.
Identifiers: LCCN: 2025918125 | ISBN: 979-8-9888921-0-6 (hardcover) | 979-8-9888921-1-3 (ebook)
Subjects: LCSH Kindness--Fiction. | Friendship--Fiction. | Community--Fiction. | BISAC FICTION / Literary | FICTION / Friendship | FICTION / Family Life / General
Classification: LCC PS3619 .A67 S65 2025 | DDC 813.6--dc23

Published by Joe Sanseverino
Clark, New Jersey

Printed in the United States of America.

Library of Congress Control Number: 2025918125
ISBN: 979-8-9888921-0-6

First edition
10 9 8 7 6 5 4 3 2 1

*Even the smallest kindness can float further
than we ever imagined.*

Dedication

This is for the quiet ones.
For the ones who listen.
For the ones making a difference
without needing to be seen.

To my family – for being my foundation.

To my wife – for being my biggest supporter.

To my sons – always carry kindness and remember what's important.

And to all those who are no longer with us –
we carry them forward in the stories we tell and the memories we keep. And because of this, they're never truly gone.

Footsteps drummed along the sidewalk as strangers brushed past. The air smelled faintly of roasted peanuts, and the distant honk of cars carried on the breeze.

Tucked between two trees sat a worn bench.
It had been there for quite some time,
but few people ever noticed it was there.

Like most things, it faded into the rhythm of the bustling city.

Its most loyal visitor was a man known as Mr. Smiles. He had glistening silver hair and a smile like sunshine. Though he was a man of simple means, he was always impeccably dressed.

He sometimes chatted,
but mostly offered a listening ear.

The world had grown loud.
And so people grew louder –
wanting to be seen, to be heard.

But under the noise,
there were hearts still quietly breaking,
and dreams that never made it past the front door.

So he'd listen.
And be as still as a pond on a peaceful day.

As he sat on the bench, he observed the hectic pace threaded into everyday routines. Illusions of connectedness disguising shadows of solitude.

That's why three ordinary objects were so important to Mr. Smiles:

a tarnished pen,
a broken watch,
and a yellow smiley face balloon.

They didn't look like much to others, but to him, they held everything that truly mattered most.

There was a time when these things didn't mean anything to him.

His pockets were empty and his days felt the same.

He moved quickly, chasing success,
trying to prove he belonged.
Running after an idea of happiness that wasn't his own.

As he'd come to realize,
life had a way of slowing things down
exactly when it was needed most.

That's when he found the watch.
Then the pen.
And one day, by way of serendipity:
the balloon.

Each one reminded him of something
he didn't want to forget again.

The pen was a gift from his father,
a teacher who spent years lighting minds and hearts.

He used to say that words were powerful enough to rekindle a torch that had burned out long ago.

Each day,
before the ink flowed onto the page,
he traced his fingers along the engraved words:
"Ignite hearts."

It reminded him that the pen wasn't just a means to tell a story. It was a tool that could spark something long after its ink had dried:

Courage.
Kindness.
Dreams.

The broken watch he wore was a gift from someone he loved deeply.

Before setting it on his wrist, he flipped the watch over and traced his fingers along the engraved words: **"Make it count."**

Even though the hands of the watch no longer moved, he still wore it.

Not to count the hours,
but to remember the brevity of time.

Everyone's watch will stop ticking someday –
a cliff of truth that helped him choose what really mattered, and move forward with steady urgency.

The smiley face balloon came from a little party shop.
A simple thing, really.

But when he held it,
people paused.
Children giggled.
And the world felt a little lighter.

Mr. Smiles gave so many balloons he lost count,
but he remembered every light they kindled.

He would often say his pen, his watch,
and the smiley face balloon were his armor:
a safeguard against *The Thieves of Peace and Joy.*

The Thieves weren't real; they were more like feelings.

The kind that slip into your mind
like a cold draft under a door.

Among them were whispers of doubt,
and the heavy hands of fear and guilt.

They were unrelenting, slowly creeping in
like rust finding its way across iron.

But over time he learned their tricks and how to deal with them.

And so, he did his best to share his invisible armor with those who needed it most.

Every day, just before noon,
Mr. Smiles made his way past the hum of the café,
through the laughter of the park,
to a place where peace and joy were harder to find:
the city hospital.

He visited everyone,
from the oldest hearts to the smallest hands.
One room in particular would become his favorite.

In Room 305, there was a young girl named Lily.

She watched the world from her window –
yellow taxis, flocks of pigeons,
and the sky painting pictures in slow motion.

She was tired.
Small.
Brave.

She hadn't smiled in a while,
but her eyes still searched for light.

Mr. Smiles handed Lily a yellow smiley face balloon,
and as he did, she felt the warmth of his presence
inside it.

The bright balloon hovered next to her,
like a tiny sun she could carry through the dark.

And for the first time in a long time,
she found her smile again.

He returned each day with a balloon in one hand,
and an adventure story in the other.

It was her favorite part of the day.
A time when she could escape from reality
and let her mind run free.

The balloon tugged at the ceiling
as if it were lifting Lily
to a land of far-off wonders.

The sterile white walls around her became a canvas for the brushstrokes of her imagination.

Lily's room transformed with every story Mr. Smiles told.

One day Lily swung on thick vines to escape monsters in the forbidden forest.

The next, she dove off a pirate ship and splashed into the sparkling blue sea.

But her favorite adventure of all was drifting weightlessly through space, scooping twinkling stars to tuck safely in her pocket.

Like clockwork, Mr. Smiles arrived for his visit with Lily, but this time something felt different.

His steps were slower.
His smile was heavier.

"Are you feeling okay?" Lily asked.

He took a deep breath.

"I'm just a little tired. You know it's hard work finding good adventure stories for you," he said, his laughter fraying into coughs.

"We can always read the book tomorrow," Lily said, her brows creasing with worry.

"I was going to tell you one of my own stories today. One about fire... and thieves. But it's okay if you don't want to hear it."

Lily's concern shifted to curiosity.

"Since you're already here, maybe I can just listen to the beginning."

They shared a laugh, and Mr. Smiles settled into the chair beside her bed.

His voice started coming more alive as he shared his story. He spoke about an inner flame we all carry inside and the forces that try to snuff it out.

"*The Thieves of Peace and Joy* will try to take anyone's flame, no matter your age," he said.

As he was telling the story, he looked out the window, almost as if seeing memories unfold in the clouds.
Like he was remembering something...
or someone.

That night she lay awake in her bed, blankly staring into the darkness.

Lily usually fell asleep watching the balloon sway above her, like a lullaby easing her to sleep.

Her thoughts, however, kept returning to Mr. Smiles.

He always took care of others,
but who was taking care of him?

She drifted off to sleep with that one question replaying in her mind.

Around noon, Lily listened for her favorite sound –
the clank of Mr. Smiles' dress shoes echoing in the halls.

She stared at the clock
watching the minutes crawl by.

12:07
12:33
1:00

The ticking grew louder,
each stroke spilling into the empty hallway.

There were no footsteps.

No yellow balloon.

The next morning, Lily slowly opened her eyes.

The smiley balloon tied beside her bed had drooped down, and its shine was a little dimmer.

By the afternoon, her face was heavy with concern.

Lily scanned the sidewalk below for any sign of Mr. Smiles.

"Where are you?" she whispered, tracing raindrops on the glass.

Still there was no speck of yellow,
no bouncing balloon.

Just an endless stream of gray umbrellas.

One of the nurses, Clara, stepped into the room for her usual check-in.

Lily was slumped by the window, lost in thought.

Clara asked, "How are we doing today, Ms. Lily?"

After a long pause, Clara broke the silence.

"If you're worried about your friend, I'm sure he'll be back soon."

Lily turned and asked, "Have you seen him?"

Clara's smile faltered. "Not today, sweetie. Maybe tomorrow."

Lily pressed her forehead against the cold glass, her breath creating a foggy haze of the outside world.

Then suddenly, a yellow balloon flashed upward, brushing past the outside corner of her window.

Her heart leapt. "He's back!"

She frantically wiped the condensation to see where he was.

But there was no sign of Mr. Smiles – just a tearful child whose balloon had slipped from his grip.

Then she noticed something strange.

There was a sea of yellow balloons gathered at the hospital entrance.

One by one,
dozens of people from all over the city stepped inside.

Behind them floated a parade of smiley face balloons.

Each one a thank you,
a memory,
a small act of kindness returned.

Mrs. Green from the party shop came first,
clutching a bundle of balloons.

She remembered how not too long ago,
Mr. Smiles had helped her liven up the store's window display.

The baker followed,
recalling sleepy mornings when Mr. Smiles brought coffee and stayed without needing a reason.

A few paces behind her was the jogger,
thankful for all the cold water bottles Mr. Smiles had
waiting for him during blistering hot days.

Then the flower lady,
with arms full of yellow daisies.

She remembered when he bought every bouquet,
during a time when her business was struggling.

Others soon followed –
a librarian,
who had her next book in hand when he asked,
"Any new adventures today?"

A bus driver,
who never forgot his friendly wave.

Neighbors and strangers alike stood shoulder to shoulder, grateful to have known the gift of true kindness.

Kindness bound by love, not expectations.

It was in that moment they understood that even the smallest kindness can spark change
beyond what the eye can see.

With a nurse steady at her side,
Lily slowly walked down the hall.

One hand held the nurse's arm; the other gripped a smiley balloon that confidently sailed alongside her.

The balloon's soft glow stood in defiance of the harsh fluorescent lights that bleached the plain walls. A subtle aroma of fresh flowers mingled with the sharp scent of sanitizer.

She tightly wrapped the balloon's string around two fingers as they neared the door.

When they reached Room 214, Lily paused.

She felt her heart tapping against her hospital gown.

The door was open just a crack,
but she couldn't see inside.

Then a terrifying thought struck:

What if he wasn't smiling?
What if... he'd lost his smile?

The nurse gave Lily a soft nod, gesturing for her to enter the room.

Inside, Mr. Smiles was resting.

He was tired.
Pale.
Weak.

"Mr. Smiles?" Lily's voice barely rose above the beeping machines.

He rolled his head toward the door,
peering through half-open eyes.

When he saw Lily, his eyes warmly crinkled and a smile broke through like the sun behind rain clouds.

"You gave me this," she whispered, tying the balloon to his bed.

"Now it's here for you."

She pulled up a chair beside Mr. Smiles, opened an adventure book, and began to read out loud.

In the days that followed,
yellow balloons appeared in every hallway.
Cards and flowers piled up on the tray table.
Laughter and lightness filled every crevice of the hospital.

Kindness coming full circle.

One bright spring morning,
Mr. Smiles returned to his familiar spot –
a little slower,
but still smiling.

The old bench had been replaced with a new one.

One that would hold the weight of new memories and kindness yet to come.

As the sun peeked through the trees,
its light caught the plaque embedded in its backrest –
almost as if the sky were placing a spotlight on it.

Before taking a seat,
he traced his fingers along the engraved words:

"In Honor of Mr. Smiles –
Ignite hearts. Make it count. Lift kindly."

He let those words sink in before carefully lowering himself to sit.

Once unnoticed, the bench now shone in its own quiet way. It became a place to return to when the world felt heavy. Its very presence offered a silent reminder to all who passed.

Sliding his hand into his coat pocket,
he pulled out his tarnished pen and a small notebook.

He breathed in the sweet scent of cherry blossoms
and began to write.

Mr. Smiles returned to the new bench year after year,
warming its seat with every story,
every moment,
every smile.

He left the world a little lighter,
and countless hearts a little brighter.

Some say Mr. Smiles changed the people he met.
Others say the people he met changed him.

Either way, the stories remain
and are told when the time feels right.

Kindness doesn't end with one person.

It spreads –
like a balloon on the breeze,
like a flame passed from one torch to another,
like a story told at just the right moment.

So long as someone is willing to carry it forward,
it never truly fades.

It started with Mr. Smiles.
And it found its way here.

And maybe, just maybe,
it found its way to you.

"The end," the teacher says, closing the book.

A child raises her hand.

"Yes, Brittany?"

"Ms. Lily... it's funny. You have the same name as the little girl in the story."

She smiles, clearing the emotion from her throat. "Curious, isn't it?"

Outside, a breeze stirred the trees, and the wind chimes sang softly through the rustling leaves.

Just beyond the window, a single yellow balloon floated toward the clouds.

And in that moment,
the world felt a little lighter.

"A generous person will prosper; whoever refreshes others will be refreshed." — Proverbs 11:25

Author's Note

I wrote *The Smiley Face Balloon* to invite us all to pause and consider how we might extend small acts of kindness without an audience and without expectation.

My hope was to create a short story that delivers some of life's most profound reminders, wrapped in an emotional, heartwarming package.

It can be something to return to when life feels heavy. Or it can be kept on a shelf or table, where its presence offers a quiet message – just like the new bench at the end of the book.

May these pages encourage you to tend your inner flame and to lift, in even the smallest ways, the people beside you.

And as you go, I invite you to share your own story of kindness or resilience. Who knows? You may just become someone's Mr. Smiles.

Keep your flame burning bright,

Joe

Share your story, and discover simple ways
to pay it forward at:
theflamekeeperseries.com

"Unexpected kindness is the most powerful, least costly, and most underrated agent of human change." — *Bob Kerrey*

Kindness Around the World

Mr. Smiles reminded us that even the smallest kindness can float farther than we ever imagined.

But kindness doesn't live only in stories. It has been etched in the slab of society, encoded in the DNA of mankind and carried across the world in countless ways.

Here are some real-life examples of how kindness has left its mark and an invitation to create your own mark of kindness.

"No one is useless in this world who lightens the burdens of another." — Charles Dickens

1. The Repair Café

In neighborhoods across the world, tables are set with tools, sewing kits, and spare parts. From broken bikes to ripped clothing, volunteers gather to fix just about anything people bring in.

It all started with one woman, Martine Postma. She had a dream to reduce waste while helping neighbors rely on each other again.

In 2009, she opened the very first Repair Café. The idea took root and spread swiftly from one community to the next.

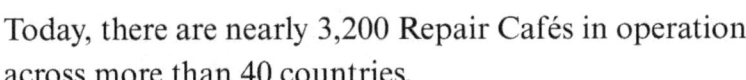

Today, there are nearly 3,200 Repair Cafés in operation across more than 40 countries.

It's a success story of kindness, showing that we can all lighten the burdens of others by putting our skills to good use. And as we mend what is broken, we find that hearts are mended too.

"Kind words can be short and easy to speak, but their echoes are truly endless." — Mother Teresa

2. The Kindness Rocks

Along quiet sidewalks and sandy beaches, colorful rocks began to appear.

Painted on them were simple messages of kindness:
"You are loved."
"Keep going."
"You are not alone."

It began in 2015, when a woman named Megan Murphy placed painted rocks along a beach in Cape Cod, Massachusetts.

Her hope was simple: that someone might find one at just the right moment and feel their day grow brighter.

The idea spread quickly. Before long, entire communities joined together to paint their own rocks of encouragement.

Each rock carries a reminder that kindness can be found in the most ordinary places – and that even the smallest words can change the course of someone's day.

*"In a place where healing is the goal,
kindness should be the method."*

3. The Healing Clowns

Hospitals can feel cold and heavy. In the 1800s, a French trio known as the Fratellini Brothers set out to change that.

Their mission was to visit hospitalized children and bring lightness where there was heaviness, and joy where there was pain.

The practice returned a century later, when an American physician named Patch Adams began clowning for patients in the 1970s. He believed that humor and human connection were as essential to healing as medicine itself.

His life's mission gained worldwide attention in the 1998 film *Patch Adams*, where Robin Williams brought his story to the screen.

Michael Christensen of the Big Apple Circus carried the movement forward by creating the first professional program of "clown doctors" in New York City, a model that soon spread across the world.

Their work is a reminder that kindness can lift hearts, even in the heaviest places.

"If you see someone alone… invite them in. That's where kindness begins."

4. The Buddy Bench

In 2013, a first grader named Christian Bucks had an idea to make sure no one felt alone at recess. He learned about a special bench at a school in Germany where children could sit if they felt lonely and wanted someone to play with.

Christian shared the idea with his principal, Matthew Miller, at Roundtown Elementary School in York, Pennsylvania.

The principal liked it so much that he had one built at their school. They called it the Buddy Bench, and soon, it caught on with other schools.

Today, thousands of schools have Buddy Benches, proving that anyone, young or old, can spread kindness.

"Even a single day of kindness can echo louder than years of conflict."

5. The Christmas Truce

In 1914, the world was at war.

But on Christmas Eve, soldiers from both sides set down their weapons and stepped out of the trenches.

They shared songs. They shared food. Some even shared a game of soccer.

For one night, the battlefield was quiet, but the message for the world would ring out loud: even kindness can shine in the darkest places.

"Carry out a random act of kindness, with no expectation of reward." — *Princess Diana*

Kindness takes many shapes.
A bench in a schoolyard.
A painted rock in the sand.
A soccer ball on a war-torn battlefield.

Some acts are small.
Some change the course of history.
But all of them remind us:
kindness is never wasted.

Like a flame passed from one torch to another,
or a balloon drifting in the wind –
it spreads from one heart to another.

And the next kindness the world remembers,
just might begin with you.

*Share your story of kindness or resilience.
Discover simple ways to pay it forward at:
theflamekeeperseries.com*

Reader's Reflection

A 3-Minute Pause

1. Sit comfortably in a quiet place.
2. Name one thing you're grateful for today.
3. Name one person you want to support.
4. Choose one small act of kindness you can do in the next 24 hours.

Four Ways to Practice Kindness

The Pen — *ignite hearts*
- Write a short note for someone (text, card, or email).
  - What do you appreciate about this person?
  - What strengths do you see in them?
  - What's one memory that stands out?

The Watch — *make it count*
- Notice the people, places, or feelings that might otherwise slip past you.
- What's one thing you'll say yes to (what matters) and one thing you'll say no to (what distracts you)?

The Balloon — *lift kindly*
- Do one small lift: hold a door, share a joke, carry a bag, bring a flower, or leave a kind comment.

The Bench — *listen deeply*
- Invite someone to tell you about their day.
- Be fully present; no multitasking and no distractions of any kind.
- Listen without fixing, comparing, or turning the story back to you.

Coming soon from *The Flamekeeper Series*:

The Flamekeeper's Guide
*A companion journal of conversations,
reflections, and courage for growing hearts.*

Scan the QR or visit: theflamekeeperseries.com/guide

Reader's Reflection

Discussion & Journal Prompts

1. How can you ignite hearts through the way you live or act?
2. Where in your day could you trade distraction for presence?
3. Who is your Lily; someone you show up for often?
4. When has someone "shown up" for you? How did it make you feel?
5. What does it mean to choose what you give importance to? What are some things you give importance to that may not truly matter?
6. How can you make things lighter around you?
7. Where is the "bench" in your life – a place to pause and reflect?
8. What does it mean to move forward with steady urgency?
9. What would giving back look like in your family, school, or neighborhood?
10. Write a life motto you'd engrave on your own bench (max 12 words).
11. Lily transforms from the listener to the storyteller. The old bench went from being unnoticeable to shining in its own way. What do these transformations mean to you?

For Groups (classrooms, book clubs, chaplaincy)

- Begin with a 3-minute pause.
  Read one scene aloud and sit in silence for 30 seconds.
  Close by having each person name one specific "lift"– a small, time-bound act of kindness they'll do before meeting again.

The Flamekeeper Series: Book 2

Kindness isn't the only thing that moves quietly through the world.

There are whispers too. Small, sneaky voices that try to dim the flame we all carry inside.

They are called *The Thieves of Peace and Joy*.
And though they visit everyone, we are not powerless against them.

Flickers of the Flame brings the series full circle, exploring life's most profound reminders wrapped once again in a heartwarming package.

Step into the story: **theflamekeeperseries.com**

www.ingramcontent.com/pod-product-compliance
Lightning Source LLC
Chambersburg PA
CBHW050521100526
44581CB00002B/59